AF708338

About the Author

Tim Cornish graduated from the London School of Economics with an honours degree in economics and later obtained an MBA from Bradford University. His early career was spent in business, in the UK and later, in the Middle East and Far East, in sales, marketing and general management positions.

At the age of forty he returned to the UK to establish a management consultancy practice which specialised in providing strategic and business development advice to legal and financial firms throughout the UK. He worked in that capacity for some twenty-five years before formally retiring in 2015.

Working alongside people in the legal and financial sectors built his respect for their professionalism and also developed his own knowledge of the issues on which they advise their clients, who are generally lay people in matters of law and finance.

However, it illustrated a conundrum in a system which, by its nature, demands a fair degree of specialisation. The more specific the problem or issue facing an individual the more he or she requires specialist advice – the more specialist the adviser the less likely it is that the recipient also receives relevant ancillary but more general advice from which they might benefit.

There is therefore a need for those approaching or already in old age, the over 50's if you like, for a holistic approach to complement the specialist approach - thus providing that sector of the population with relevant and appropriate overall legal, financial and related issues they may or will face.

LifeHolder has been written to help empower the lay person by providing such a holistic overview. Its aim is to increase knowledge and awareness of these issues so that they may be recognised and subsequently managed, mitigated or alleviated by consulting an appropriate specialist.

UPFRONT PUBLISHING

LifeHolder

ISBN: 978-178456-609-6

Perfect Bound

First published 2013 by Upfront Publishing, Peterborough, England
This edition published in 2020 also by Upfront Publishing

An environmentally friendly book printed and bound in England
by www.printondemand-worldwide.com

Preface

This book is called **Life**Holder because it's about the life you hold - your own.

It's about helping you plan for your later life, so that you can best enjoy the years of retirement.

It's about helping you plan for the inevitable end of life and helping you cope with what may be a considerable prior period when you may need the help of those close to you, as well perhaps of others too.

It's also about the certainty of death and the probability of incapacity of some degree prior to that, since medical science has become so adept at prolonging our lives and postponing eventual death.

As human beings we have a tendency to avoid thinking about difficult issues, often preferring to put them off until tomorrow, and repeating that postponement again and again, sometimes until it is too late.

The purpose of this book is to help you overcome that natural reluctance, to encourage you to consider and then to act, so that you will enjoy the peace of mind of knowing that you will have done the best for yourself and the best for those whom you care most about.

Contents

Introduction

LifeHolder has been written for the layman, as a convenient guide to those personal matters which should be contemplated and considered in middle and later life.

Much as we might not like to think about it we are all, one day, going to die. Most of us will leave behind friends, family and assets.

As we all know intrinsically, the appropriate and traditional way to deal with these issues is to make a **Will**. However, a Will does not deal with all the issues which arise before and after death.

Most of us also give thought to how we want our body disposed of, and a few of us how we would like our passing to be marked, by making an **Advance Funeral Directive**.

Some of us also contemplate how our death might help others live by registering our wish for **Organ** or **Tissue Donation**. And a small number of us consider **Body Donation** for teaching or medical research so that future generations may benefit.

As medical science advances and increases our life expectancies many of us will, sadly, at some stage lose mental or physical capacity. These situations can be mitigated, to the benefit of family, friends, carers and medical staff as well as to ourselves if we consider, in advance, instruments such as **Lasting Powers of Attorney** and/or an **Advance Decision (Living Will)**.

Financial matters should also concern us as we approach retirement and old age. Most of us will wish to maximise the net wealth we leave behind, whether that is to benefit our children, friends, or favourite charities. This may require **Tax and Estate Planning**.

Some of us may end up with inadequate income to fund our lifestyles and will need to look at sources of finance such as **Equity Release**.

A significant, and increasing, proportion of us can contemplate needing some form of **Residential Care** in the last part of our lives. All of us need to look at the potential cost of such care and the effect it will have financially and emotionally, on our families.

LifeHolder deals simply and briefly with all of these issues and others, not in a technical or detailed way, but by raising awareness which, hopefully, will prompt readers to seek the necessary professional and other advice in their own, and their family's interests.

Part A –
Planning for the Inevitable

In this section we look at death and how to plan for its consequences. In particular, we look at how to minimise the distress and discomfort of relatives and friends by making a **Will** and how **Will Registration** can help avoid the potential problem of 'missing Wills'.

We also look at the advantages of making an **Advance Funeral Directive** and consider the issues and practicalities of **Organ** and **Body Donation**.

1. Making a Will

The cornerstone of planning for death is making a Will. Statistics show that only some 30% of the UK population get round to taking the necessary action – so that in 7 out of 10 deaths no express wishes have been recorded by the deceased – causing distress, often disharmony, and worry to those left behind.

Why you should make a Will

If you die without making a Will (known as dying intestate) the law will decide how your estate is distributed, in accordance with long established statutory intestacy rules. These rules are very unlikely to coincide with your own wishes. So there are a number of very good reasons for making a Will:

- You retain control by planning ahead
- You get to choose who receives what, not someone else
- You can provide for your loved ones
- You can mitigate the tax payable on your estate
- You can minimise the distress of those you leave behind
- You can choose your own executor(s)

Dying intestate invariably causes problems for the family, particularly where the deceased had been married more than once and there are children and/ or stepchildren from more than one of those relationships. The intestacy rules are simply unable to cope adequately with that type of circumstance.

The notes below have been designed to offer some initial guidance so that you can consider the most important aspects of making a Will, collect your thoughts, and perhaps discuss the issues with your family.

This process will result in a reasonably clear idea of what you want to do. It will facilitate discussion with your solicitor, who will be able to help fill in the details and offer the most practical advice on how your wishes can be accommodated, in the most convenient, straightforward and cost-efficient way.

Matters for Consideration

The following are important matters you should give thought to:

Children

If you have children under the age of 18 your surviving spouse or partner will probably continue to care for them. However you should consider appointing guardians in the event you and your spouse/partner die at the same time – it can happen! This will require some deep thought and discussion with the person or persons you want to appoint, so that everyone feels comfortable about the arrangement.

You may also want to provide for monies to be invested until your children reach the age of 18 (or older, if you wish). If you have a child who is disadvantaged or disabled you will be particularly concerned to make adequate arrangements for their welfare and well-being after your death.

Inheritance Tax & Estate Planning

You do not have to be very wealthy to be caught in the inheritance tax net (see Section 1 in Part C). With the majority of people now owning their own home, and with the value of those homes in many cases exceeding the tax threshold, many estates will attract IHT.

However, there are a number of legitimate means to avoid or mitigate the effect of this tax. Your solicitor and/or financial adviser can advise you on these and help you choose the most effective means to suit your circumstances.

Executors

An executor is someone, nominated by the person making the Will, who will have the responsibility of administering the estate after death. You need to decide who you wish to deal with your estate and carry out the instructions specified in your Will. This should be someone who knows you and whom you can trust. (You can nominate someone who is also a beneficiary of you Will if you wish.)

Because some estates can prove to be quite complicated, many people choose to appoint a professional person, such as a solicitor, as a joint (or sole) executor. This is a safeguard and can be useful where your other chosen executor is a lay person. You should note, however, that a professional person so appointed will make a charge for their services in this regard.

Physical Assets & Liabilities

In order to draw up your Will you will need to consider what you will leave behind (referred to as your estate).

You should draw up an initial list of all your physical assets – these include your house, your investments and savings including any shares you hold, bank accounts, insurance policies and pension funds as well as family heirlooms, antiques etc.

There may be liabilities which you currently have, such as a mortgage. These need to be totaled and the amount deducted from assets to give a figure for your approximate net assets. A precise valuation is not required but your solicitor/financial adviser will need to know the general order so they can advise on minimising any tax liabilities your estate may attract.

Digital Assets

Not so long ago, before we all had a mobile phone, laptop, tablet or personal computer we had no digital assets. Now, most of us have such assets, which may have Financial, Social or Sentimental value.

- Assets with Financial value include online bank accounts, savings accounts, shopping accounts, loyalty or reward cards and even, perhaps, cryptocurrencies.
- Assets with Social value include memberships of Twitter, Facebook, LinkedIn and others.
- Assets with Sentimental value include photographs and videos stored on our phone or computer (or in the cloud) and other files in Word, Excel or any other format.

Financial assets which are owned by you obviously have value and can therefore be bequeathed. Social or Sentimental assets may be cherished but may not be legally owned by you if the terms and conditions of the 'hosting platform or platforms' claim ownership.

The law concerning digital assets is new and developing, and detailed advice is beyond the scope of this publication. However it is suggested that you draw up and maintain a 'Digital Asset Directory' listing your digital assets and where they are held, together with your passwords so that they may be accessed by your executor(s) after your death. In the Directory you should also indicate what your wishes are regarding the disposal or passing on of the assets.

N.B. The Directory itself must NOT be made part of your Will, as that becomes a public document on your death. Instead, keep it in a safe place and ensure that your family and executor(s) are aware of its existence and location.

Your Wishes

Sometimes the most difficult part of the exercise is to decide how you want your estate to be distributed after your death. Possible beneficiaries include your spouse, your children, your grandchildren, any siblings, nephews and nieces.

In addition to family you may also wish to leave legacies to godchildren, friends, charities or other bodies.

If you have been married more than once and if you have children from one or more of the marriages you will need to consider how you wish to have them benefit from your estate. The situation is further complicated if your spouse or partner also has children from a previous marriage, and will need discussion between all parties.

You also need to consider how you want the beneficiaries to benefit – via specified amounts (e.g. £1000) or by proportion (e.g. half of my estate) or via specific item (e.g. my wristwatch to my grandson). In almost all instances there is a residue after the specific bequests have been made. Whom do you wish to receive this residue?

Remember there is always the possibility that one or more of your beneficiaries may die before you. You should therefore give some thought to alternatives.

Reviewing Your Will

You should note that it is very important to review your Will from time to time, every few years at least.

Your circumstances may change, your family and friends may grow or contract, or the law may change in a way which requires changes to your arrangements to ensure they remain tax efficient and correspond with your wishes.

Your Digital Asset Directory may need more frequent review and update, particularly if you are a regular user of the internet, social media and the like.

A Note on Ownership of Foreign Property

Increasing numbers of us are realising their dreams by investing in foreign property, either to have a holiday home in the sun or as an eventual retirement home.

However, most foreign countries have succession laws which are very different from our own, a fact which makes it difficult in all cases (and impossible in most) to deal with the eventual disposal of the property in a Will drawn up under English law.

The issue can be quite complex and requires legal advice. You should seek professional advice to deal with this issue if you have, or are contemplating purchasing, a property overseas.

2. Registering Your Will

It is a sad fact that, every year, a proportion of those who die having made a Will, in fact die intestate, because the Will is never found.

It is traditional in the UK for solicitors to retain the original copy of each Will they draw up on behalf of their clients – the vast majority of firms offer this as a free service. However, although Wills may be safely and securely stored in this way, they can only be used for the purpose intended, if the solicitor concerned is informed that the person has died!

Sadly, in a significant number of deaths each year, the family and friends of the deceased are unaware of the existence or location of a Will. The result is that the Will may not be found, with the consequence that the estate has to be wound up (and distributed) according to the rules of intestacy. This means that the testator's wishes, as expressed in the Will, will not be carried out. Family, friends, charities, and other potential beneficiaries may not then receive the inheritances that the testator wished them to have.

Fortunately there is now a national Will Register which can help ensure that Wills are found after the testator dies.

The Will Register is called Certainty and can be found at www.certainty.co.uk. Registration can be done simply and quickly for a small one-off fee, either by the solicitor acting for the testator, or the testator themselves.

Only the name of the testator, the date and the location of the original Will are required for registration. The relationship between solicitor and testator and the contents of the Will itself remain confidential, but the register can be searched by someone seeking the whereabouts of a Will after the death of the testator.

Anyone who then approaches the solicitor holding the Will would have to demonstrate their credentials and their right to have possession of the document, in the normal way.

3. Types of Funeral

Not knowing what the deceased would have wanted; in respect of the funeral service (music, readings, hymns etc.); in respect of disposal of the body (burial or cremation); and sometimes whether or not they would have wanted to donate any of their organs can cause the greatest anguish and worry to those left behind.

This section considers the topic of funeral planning, and the importance of making your family aware of your wishes.

It also looks at the different types of funeral that are now possible.

Conventional Funerals

Religious Funerals
The vast majority of funerals in the UK are conducted in accordance with tradition with some form of religious ceremony and about 70% are cremations, with most of the remainder being burials in a churchyard or cemetery

Non-Religious Funerals
For those who have lived their life without religion it is possible to have a non-religious ceremony. The charity Humanists UK, for example, offers a service whereby a trained officiant will conduct a non-religious ceremony celebrating the life of the deceased.

Non-Conventional Funerals

Family-led Funerals
In recent years a new trend has emerged whereby the funeral ceremony is run by a member (or members) of the family. As well as reducing costs this enables the eulogy to be delivered by someone who knew the deceased rather than a priest or professional officiant who did not.

Traditionally, after the funeral celebration, the body is disposed of by cremation or burial in a churchyard or local authority graveyard. However, if this is not what you want there are other alternatives:

Direct Cremation

Here the body is disposed of at the crematorium, without any ceremony and with no family or friends present. The ashes are later returned to the relatives, who may hold a scattering ceremony, a traditional wake, or other memorial event in a place of their choosing.

The cost, usually between £1200 and £1500, is about a third of that for a conventional crematorium funeral. This 'no-frills' service has become popular in recent years and is now offered by many funeral directors, including the largest ones.

Burial at Sea

It is possible to be buried at sea, although this is not encouraged by the authorities. There are three licensed locations in England - off Newhaven, Sussex or The Needles, Isle of Wight, or Tynemouth, Northumbria. Just 50 or so non-navy burials at sea are granted each year by the Marine Management Organisation, which is part of the Department of Environment & Rural Affairs, to whom initial application has to be made - see Part F for details.

An embalmed body cannot be buried at sea (embalming chemicals might, over time, contaminate the water). Therefore if this is an option you want you should make sure that family members are aware of your wishes so that undertakers do not embalm your body.

Natural Burial (in non-consecrated ground)

An alternative to burial in a churchyard or cemetery is burial in non-consecrated ground. Such burials have long been possible and there are now around 200 woodland burial sites in the UK which offer this alternative to cemeteries. They are managed privately (often by farmers) or by a local authority.

There are no gravestones or other signs or monuments. Burial sites are either left unmarked, or are marked by the planting of a tree or wild flowers.

As with burial at sea, the body must not be embalmed, in order to prevent possible contamination of the watercourse. Also, for such burials, any coffin used must be made from a fully degradable material such as cardboard or wicker, or a cloth or drape used instead.

The Association of Natural Burial Grounds, formed by The Natural Death Centre in 1994, contains a national listing of sites run by its members. Further information can be found by contacting The Natural Death Centre – see Part F for details .

4. Advance Funeral Directives

If you want to ensure you have the funeral ceremony which you want, with the music, poems, readings etc. of your choice you should make your immediate family aware, so that they can begin to carry out your wishes immediately after your death, before any irreversible actions are taken.

The best way of ensuring your wishes are carried out is to make an Advance Funeral Wish or Directive. Making such a directive means that you decide what you would like and those who you leave behind are spared from having to make the (sometimes difficult) decisions which arise, and having to guess what you might have wanted.

The Directive can be a fairly simple document stating your preference as to cremation or burial and perhaps nominating the hymns or other music you would like played. However, it can be as comprehensive as you like and go down to such details as to who you want to be bearers of your coffin, where and how you would like the news of your death to be announced, and so on.

A downloadable, very detailed format, of an Advance Funeral Directive can be downloaded, free of charge, from the Bereavement Advice Centre – See Part F for details.

If you do draw up a Directive the key thing is to let your near family know that you have and where it is located so it is accessed quickly after death, thereby allowing your wishes to be carried out.

5. Organ & Tissue Donation

Every Year around 400 people die in the UK while waiting while waiting for a lung, liver, kidney or heart transplant.

There is a critical shortage of organs and the gap between the number of organs donated and the number of people waiting for a transplant is increasing. According to NHS statistics, at any time more than 7000 people in the UK need an organ transplant. It is a paradox that as medical science advances and makes more transplants possible, with increasing chances of success, the gap grows.

Organs that can be donated after death include the heart, lungs, kidneys, liver, pancreas and small bowel. Tissues such as skin, bone, heart valves and corneas can also be used to help others.

Eligibility for donation

Virtually anyone can elect, and be accepted, to be a donor.

Age is not a barrier. In the case of cornea and some other tissue age is not a factor at all. For other transplants it is the person's physical condition which is the crucial factor. Successful transplants have been achieved from donors in their 70's and 80's.

Ethnicity is not a barrier. On the contrary the more diverse the backgrounds of potential donors on the Register the better, since organs are matched by blood group and tissue type, meaning that patients from the same ethnic group are more likely to make a close match.

Even potential donors with an existing medical condition can be accepted. A decision about whether particular organs are suitable is made, at the time of death, by doctors taking account of the person's medical history. In most cases it is possible for some organs to be donated.

None of the major religions in the UK object to the concept of organ or tissue donation. However, if you are in any doubt you should discuss the matter with your spiritual or religious adviser.

Becoming a Donor (Opt-Out or Opt-In)

For many years the NHS has successfully operated an Organ Donation Register on an Opt-In basis, i.e. where individuals have to opt to become donors on their own volition.

You can join the Register by calling 0300 123 23 23, or visiting their website which is found at www.uktransplant.org.uk. (It is also possible to register when applying for a driving license, or when registering at a GP surgery.) In addition to being placed on the Register you will receive a donor card which you can carry with you.

As well as potentially helping others to live or improve their lives, becoming a donor can also help your family. They may be faced with having to decide whether to accede to a request for organ or tissue donation after your death – making such a decision would be so much easier if they knew, in advance, what your wishes would have been.

Despite the success of this Opt-In scheme it has long been held by the medical profession that an Opt-Out scheme, if adopted, would result in more successful transplants and thus more lives being saved. Such a scheme would require those who did not want to be prospective donors on their death, to opt out. Those who chose not to opt out would be deemed to agree to become prospective donors.

Parliament has now passed a law to effect this change which, in England, will become effective in May 2020. The NHS has estimated that the move will save in the order of 700 additional lives per annum.

In Wales the system is already one of 'deemed consent' and in Scotland an opt-out scheme will be introduced in the autumn of 2020. Northern Ireland will continue to operate an opt-in system.

It should be noted that, both before and after the introduction of the new Opt Out scheme, your family will be consulted about donation of your organs when you have died, whether you have positively opted in by registering or whether you have not opted out. In either case, they (the family) can object if they do not wish your organs to be donated, and their position will be respected and accepted.

However, if you have registered, and have told your family that you have done so it is more likely than not that your family will not object, since you had made your wishes clear (The Organ Donation Register will continue to be maintained after spring 2020). If, therefore, you are strongly of the view that you would like your organs to be donated you would be advised to register and tell your family that you have done so.

N.B. *It will be pointless if you just express your wish to have your organs donated in your Will, as by the time that is read it will be far too late!*

6. Body Donation (for Medical Research or Training)

Over the past few years the numbers of bodies left to medical research or training has been falling – to the point where many senior doctors and surgeons are becoming very concerned.

Traditionally, medical students have learned their trade by dissecting human bodies – clearly a preferred route to performing surgery on a live person. The fall in numbers of bodies available for training purposes now means that some budding surgeons are unable to learn in this way. One leading surgeon recently stated he "found it worrying" that for a newly qualified surgeon their first incision would be made on a living person.

No bodies can be accepted for teaching purposes if organs have been removed for donation (except if only the corneas are to be donated). A body will also not be accepted if it has been subject to a post-mortem examination or the person had been severely deformed or suffered from hepatitis, dementia or severe obesity.

A bequest to leave your body for research or training must be made in writing in the presence of a witness. You should complete the necessary forms, available from your local medical school, through The Human Tissue Authority - see Part F below for further details.

N.B. *Consent must be given prior to death, it cannot be given by anyone after your death*

Part B - Potential Incapacity

Having looked at death itself we now look at the (very real) possibility that, before we die, we may suffer some serious mental or physical incapacity. Utilising a **Lasting Power of Attorney** can mitigate the distressing consequences of incapacity, to the benefit of all concerned.

If incapacity occurs and no Power of Attorney has been arranged, a **Deputyship** may need to be arranged.

Unless death comes suddenly and unexpectedly there is likely to be a period of time leading up to the event when you will need medical care. You, and those treating you, may be faced with decisions about the nature of the treatment you receive. Your ability to communicate your wishes may become impaired. We look at how an **Advance Decision** (or **Living Will**) can help in such circumstances.

1. Lasting Power of Attorney

Making a Will records one's wishes in the event of death. However, circumstances may arise before death where one becomes seriously incapacitated – to the extent that mental capacity is insufficient to make considered decisions and judgements about one's own affairs.

Commonly, diseases such as Alzheimer's and other forms of dementia overtake elderly people. But other conditions such as motor neurone disease, or indeed unexpected traumas such as accidents, can affect us at any age.

In such circumstances, where we become unable to manage our own affairs, the law adopts a protective stance. It permits no-one, not even our spouse or other near relative, access to our bank account or other financial assets without due process. That process is through the aptly named Court of Protection and involves the appointment of a Deputy. The problem is that the process is costly and protracted and, until settled, there are bills to be paid and decisions which cannot be made (see also Deputyship).

All of this can cause stress and inconvenience, to all concerned.

Fortunately there is a legal device which, if in place at the time incapacity occurs, will minimise the delay and avoid application to the Court. This device is known as a Lasting Power of Attorney (LPA).

Purpose of an LPA

An LPA is a legal document which enables you, in advance of any potential incapacity, to nominate one or more people (known as attorneys) to deal with your affairs, on your behalf, should you become prevented from doing so yourself by mental illness or disability. The vital requirement is to anticipate the possibility of future mental incapacity and draw up the document before such incapacity occurs. It is not possible to appoint an attorney after the event.

For most of us it is impossible to anticipate if or when we might succumb to mental incapacity. It is therefore prudent, particularly so when we are in middle or old age and therefore closer to the possibility, to consider making an LPA.

There are two types of LPA – one deals with Personal Welfare and the other deals with Property & Affairs.

Lasting Power of Attorney – Personal Welfare (LPA Welfare)

This allows you to appoint one or more attorneys to take decisions about your healthcare and general welfare should you lose the capacity to do so yourself.

You can specify restrictions or conditions on the decisions they may make, or you can give them general power to make any decision they may consider necessary. If you wish you can give them authority to give or refuse consent to life-sustaining treatment on your behalf.

Lasting Power of Attorney – Property & Affairs (LPA Finance)

This allows you to appoint one or more attorneys to take decisions about your property and financial affairs, should you lose the capacity to do so yourself.

As with an LPA Welfare you can specify any restrictions or conditions you wish, or you can give them general authority to deal with your affairs.

Benefits of an LPA

An LPA has a number of advantages; it enables you to retain control of your affairs (by proxy), it helps guarantee your future security, and it can relieve your family/friends of distress and worry. By setting up an LPA you create a legal framework that will allow your affairs to be administered by someone of your own choosing who you know and trust, should you be prevented from acting on your own behalf sometime in the future.

In the event you are rendered incapable of administering your own affairs, and you have not set up an LPA (Finance), your estate and your financial affairs will be managed by the Court of Protection who will arrange for a Deputy to be appointed.

Making an LPA (Welfare) gives you control by proxy over your medical treatment and care by doctors, nurses, social workers and carers, even if you lose capacity, because you stated your preferences in writing whilst you were capable. If you have not done this you will have no control over any decisions they may take. (See also Advance Decision, page 24 below).

Setting up an LPA

You can make an LPA online or by using paper forms. Either way, you need to get other people to sign the forms, including the attorneys and witnesses. Although you can do it yourself, the form and procedures concerned are quite complex and many people prefer to have the benefit of professional advice and help.

You should consider whether you should make both types of LPA, or whether you prefer to make arrangements for just one of the different types of issues. You may wish to discuss this with family and friends.

Appointing Attorneys – Sole, Joint, or Joint & Several?

You may decide to appoint just one attorney, or two or more. In any event they should be people you know and trust implicitly, typically close relatives. If that is not possible you should choose a professional person such as a solicitor.

If you choose to appoint just one attorney he or she will act individually on your behalf. If you choose to appoint two attorneys you can elect for them to act only jointly i.e. all decisions must be taken by both together, or jointly and severally, whereby one of the two may act independently if a decision is urgent or relatively simple, or jointly if the matter is not of immediate concern or is of greater import.

Note that if you appoint attorneys only to act jointly and one of them dies, or becomes incapacitated, the LPA will become null and void. Similarly if you appoint a sole attorney and they die or become incapacitated, the LPA will fail.

If you decide to set up both types of LPA you may wish to appoint different attorneys for each type. It may be, for example, that someone you think suitable to act on your behalf on health and welfare issues would not be suitable to deal with your financial affairs, or vice versa. If this is the case you will need different attorneys for each LPA.

You then need to think about what powers you want to give your attorney(s). You can give general powers or very limited and specific ones

Whilst virtually anyone over the age of 18 (provided they are not bankrupt) can be appointed as an attorney, in practice most will be close family members or professional advisers since they should be people you can trust implicitly.

Certificate Provider

In order to prevent fraud and to deter potential abuse of powers it is a requirement of the legislation governing LPAs that an independent person* discusses with you your intent to establish an LPA. This person, if satisfied that you understand the purpose of the LPA and that you are not being coerced or pressured to sign the form, then signs the part of the form entitled 'Statement of certificate provider'. Without such a signature the form will not be valid and the LPA will not be granted.

** The independent person can be someone who is known to you, but cannot be a relative, or your spouse or civil partner, neither can he or she be a nominated attorney, or a current paid carer, or a manager or employee of any care home where you reside, or someone named on the form as a person to be notified of the registration of the LPA. If there is no-one who you know personally outside of these categories you can discuss your intent to set up the LPA with a solicitor, barrister, bank manager, clergyman, or other professional person.*

Registering an LPA

To become effective an LPA has to be registered with the Office of the Public Guardian (OPG). This will take 11 or 12 weeks to complete but, provided application is made in good time, the LPA will be 'in place' and can be effected immediately incapacity becomes evident.

In order to help prevent fraud, the application form requires the applicant to nominate up to five different, and potentially interested persons, who are family members or otherwise close friends or associates. These persons will be contacted by the OPG, informed of the intent to appoint an attorney(s) and invited to object to that appointment, giving the reasons for such objection.

If there are any objections the OPG will consider them and make a judgement. If an objection is held to be reasonable, the proposed PLA will not be registered and therefore not become legal.

2. Deputyship

As noted above, if a person becomes incapable of handling their own affairs through some sort of incapacity, someone else has to take over.

If forethought has been applied and an attorney appointed under an LPA Finance, that attorney can (provided the LPA has been registered, as described above) immediately begin to handle the person's affairs, according to the powers given to them in the document.

By contrast, if no LPA had been established prior to the onset of incapacity, a Deputy has to be appointed by the Court of Protection to manage the affairs of the person concerned.

Dealing with the Court can be time consuming and complex – and costly. Appointment of a Deputy can take many weeks, and the person eventually appointed may be someone not even known to the incapacitated person.

The Court will determine the powers that the Deputy has in acting on the person's behalf and will grant them responsibility for property and financial affairs including maintaining a bank account, paying bills, purchasing property, and arranging finances generally. The Deputy will have to account to the Court on an annual basis. The Court will supervise the Deputy in their duties throughout the duration of the deputyship to the degree commensurate with the Court's view of their competence and experience.

Setting up an LPA has its costs, including the cost of professional advice and Court fees.

However, appointing a Deputy will undoubtedly incur larger (and ongoing) fees.

The decision, eventually for all of us, is whether to incur the relatively low costs of setting up a Lasting Power of Attorney ***before the possibility*** of incapacity, or to take the risk that incapacity will not affect us before death and that the protracted, complex and more expensive costs of having the Court of Protection appoint a Deputy (with consequent distress and inconvenience to our family) will be avoided.

3. Advance Decision (Living Will)

An Advance Decision (or Living Will) is a document which tells your doctors what kind of medical care you would like if you become unable to make decisions on your own behalf or unable to communicate your wishes (in Scotland it is known as an Advance Directive).Whereas an LPA Welfare (see above) enables you to appoint an attorney or attorneys to act on your behalf in health and welfare matters, an Advance Decision can be more specific as to the medical treatment or treatments you would wish to receive if you have lost capacity to communicate with your carers or medical advisers.

Because an Advance Decision is not a statutory document and has no defined format it can be a more flexible instrument than an LPA - it will also be less expensive to draw up.

Neither document has anything to do with the distribution of your estate after death (this is covered by your Will).

A growing number of people are choosing to make Advance Decisions because:

- You can make your own wishes clear, while you are able
- You help prevent those closest to you from having to make difficult decisions on your behalf
- You help those treating you by informing them about your wishes and absolving them from the task of guessing what you would want
- You take control of your future medical treatment

In the absence of an Advance Decision (and/or an LPA Welfare) and if you are unable to communicate your wishes, your doctors will decide what treatment they think is in your best interests. Although they may consult your next of kin or immediate family, it is they who ultimately decide what to do. If you make an Advance Decision you can set out what medical treatment you wish to accept or refuse in such circumstances.

Advance Decisions and the Law

The Mental Capacity Act 2005, which became effective on 1 October 2007, has clarified the law on Advance Decisions/Living Wills and given them legal status.

Format of an Advance Decision

There is no statutory document or defined format for an Advance Decision.

It can be a fairly simple statement of your wishes, expressed in generalities rather than specifics but which, nevertheless, give the medical team treating you a good indication of your wishes. Alternatively the document can be quite detailed, specifying what you wish in different circumstances, or for different conditions or illnesses.

You may, in the document, nominate a 'Health Care Proxy' (a position similar to an attorney appointed under an LPA-Welfare). This would typically be a close friend or relative who knows your wishes and can communicate them to the medical team on your behalf. The document should be signed by you, in the presence of (preferably) two witnesses not related to you and who do not expect to benefit from your death. It should also name your General Practitioner and give his/her contact details.

Once you have completed your Advance Decision you should ensure that all those close to you know that you have done so, and where it is located.

N.B. *If you want to refuse life-sustaining treatment in your Advance Decision you must include in the document a statement that your wishes apply to the specific treatment or treatments, even if your life is at risk.*

Professional Advice

You should certainly consult your doctor. This will help you to know exactly what the healthcare options are and, after you have drawn up the document, you should ensure he or she has a copy and a note to the effect on your medical record.

A comprehensive format for an Advance Decision can be downloaded, free of charge, from the charity Compassion in Dying - see Part F for details. See also Appendix 4 which shows an example of a simpler format.

Part C - Financial Planning

Financial planning is always important, but never more so than when contemplating your retirement, old age, and death.

When drawing up your Will **Inheritance Tax** and **Estate Planning** may need to be addressed. After retirement you may need to look at means of supplementing your retirement income by downsizing your home or taking **Equity Release**.

It is probable that at some stage in your later life you will have to go into **Residential Care** if and when you become incapable of looking after yourself. If you have even a moderate amount of savings and assets you will be required to pay for most, if not all, of your care home fees.

Perhaps you may also wish to put aside some regular savings to **Fund your Funeral** costs or for other purposes and you may also wish to consider purchasing a **Funeral Bond**.

These are mostly areas where professional advice is needed, both legal and financial, and if necessary most solicitors would expect to advise you in concert with an appropriate independent financial adviser, and vice versa.

1. Inheritance Tax & Estate Planning

Estate planning refers to the whole process of forward planning to ensure that what you want to occur after your death does indeed happen, and taking the right steps to ensure that tax payable on your estate (and therefore borne by your beneficiaries) is minimised. As such, estate planning includes the process of drawing up a Will, and including within that document appropriate devices to achieve your aims.

IHT is payable on any estate where the net value exceeds £325,000* (this figure will remain the same until 2021, after which it will increase in line with the Consumer Prices Index). The rate of tax imposed is 40% on the whole amount above the threshold (although this reduces to 36% where 10% or more of the net estate is left to charity). The inheritance tax on an estate worth £500,000 would therefore be £70,000 (40% of the taxable amount of £175,000 which is £500,000 minus £325,000).

But see also the below section on **Residence Nil Band Rate which increases the allowance beyond the £325,000 level in certain circumstances.*

When it is due IHT must be paid before probate is granted – that is, before any monies left in the Will can be distributed.

Marriage & Civil Partnership

Every person is entitled to a nil band rate for IHT (this rate is £325,000). Assets which pass from one spouse or civil partner to another are exempt from the tax. So if on death, someone leaves everything they own to their spouse or civil partner, and they have not used any of their nil band rate it is exempt from IHT.

The unused nil band rate can now be transferred to the surviving spouse or civil partner. Thus, no IHT is payable on the first death and the nil band rate on the second death will be £650,000 (2 x £325,000).

If some of the nil band rate was used on the first death, not all of the rate can be transferred. For example, if the first death occurred during 2007-08 (when the nil tax band was £300,000) and the deceased left assets worth £150,000 to the children and everything else to the spouse, one half (50%) of the nil band rate was unused and can be transferred.

If the second death occurs in 2011 (when the nil rate band is £325,000) the amount available for transfer would be 50% of £325,000, or £162,500. Therefore the tax free part of the estate of the second spouse would be £487,500 (£325,000 plus £162,500).

In contrast to people who are married or in a civil partnership, cohabiting couples cannot transfer the nil rate band on the first death. Therefore if one cohabitee leaves all their estate to the other, IHT will be payable on everything above £325,000 of the total estate on the second death (as opposed to everything above £650,000 in the case of marriage or civil partnership).

Residence Nil Rate Band (RNRB)

The RNRB applies to individuals with direct descendants who have an estate (including a main residence) that exceeds the IHT threshold of £325,000. It was introduced in tax year 2017/18 at the level of £100,000 to be increased annually at £25,000 up until tax year 2020/21 when it reaches a level of £175,000. After that time it will increase in line with the Consumer Prices Index.

To qualify for RNRB you must have an inheritance which exceeds the nil-band rate of £325,000 and you must bequeath your family home to your children or grandchildren. In those circumstances your inheritance tax threshold would increase, on April 2020 for example, from £325,000 to £500,000 (£325,000 + £175,000).

In a marriage or civil partnership each party can pass on this "revised IHT threshold" tax free, meaning that on the second death the total tax free amount will be £1 million (2 x £500,000).

Other means of reducing IHT liability

The estates of single people and divorcees will also be subject to IHT on all amounts over £325,000 (potentially enhanced by up to an additional amount of £175,000 if they can claim RNRB). For these individuals and for the very wealthy it is possible to reduce IHT liability by creating different types of trusts. Some of these are described briefly below but the legal and financial environment can be complex and is subject to change, so professional advice should always be sought. Other means of mitigating IHT include making gifts (also dealt with below).

Types of Trusts

Asset Preservation Trusts

These trusts protect pension death benefits from IHT, ensure that they are not assessed as capital should the surviving spouse require long-term care, and guarantee that the benefits pass to your children rather than your spouse's new husband or wife should they remarry.

Business Trusts

These hold life assurance arrangements by Partners or Directors to allow flexibility in ownership through death or retirement; and make sure that the surviving partners/directors have the money to buy the deceased's share of the business and ensure the deceased's beneficiaries get a fair price for the latter's share in the business.

Guardianship Protection Trusts

These trusts operate on a life assurance plan creating funds for guardians to look after orphaned children.

Gift Plan Trusts

These trusts allow investment via an Investment Bond ensuring that IHT is mitigated if the donor survives seven years since the original value of the gift (along with any growth in value) will be outside the estate.

Absolute Trusts

These allow gifts to a grandchild (for example, for school or university fees) allowing the recipient to make use of their personal tax allowance.

Life Interest Trusts

These trusts provide for a specified beneficiary to receive for life the income generated by the trust's investments, but the capital passes (on death of the recipient) to the next set of beneficiaries, for example children.

Inheritance Creation Trusts

These trusts operate on the basis of a life assurance plan (either single life or joint life second death) creating funds for anticipated IHT liability, so that the tax can be paid quickly, allowing the swift granting of probate. Alternatively the cash generated may be used to create an additional legacy.

Tax Exempt Gifts

Certain gifts are exempt from IHT and other taxes. These include:

- Anything you give your spouse or civil partner (provided he/she lives in the UK)
- Gifts to UK charities, museums, universities, the National Trust and certain other institutions
- Gifts of up to £3,000 in any one tax year
- Gifts of up to £250 to as many people as you wish
- Wedding gifts of up to £5,000 to each of your children
- Wedding gifts of up to £2,500 to each of your grandchildren
- Wedding gifts of up to £1,000 to anyone else

Larger Transfers of Capital (PETS)

HM Revenue & Customs will permit the transfer of limitless sums to UK based individuals. Such transfers are known as Potentially Exempt Transfers (PETS). 'Potentially' since they escape IHT entirely provided the donor survives for seven years.

If the donor dies at any time within the seven years tax will be payable on a sliding scale – for example, if death occurs between 3 and 4 years after donation tax will be levied at 80% of the standard rate (i.e. at 32% as opposed to 40%); if it occurs between 4 and 5 years after donation the rate falls to 60% of the standard rate (i.e. at 24% as opposed to 40%); and so on.

Clearly it is best, from the tax point of view, if such transfers are made as early in life as possible. However, you must be at a stage in life when you can reasonably judge how much you can afford to give away without depriving yourself of the lifestyle you would like!

N.B. *It is highly recommended that professional advice be taken when planning for IHT and Estate Planning generally. However, be aware that HMRC operates a free Helpline for IHT enquiries which can be utilised by members of the public - see Section F below for details.*

2. Equity Release

If you have been a home owner for a number of years it is probably worth more than you paid for it, possibly a lot more. Yet, until the concept of equity release was conceived, there was no way you could enjoy the cash that is 'locked up' in the bricks and mortar, other than to feel good in the knowledge that your children and/or grandchildren would one day inherit its value.

Now, it is very easy to release some of the equity 'residing' in your home and take it out as cash to spend on yourself - tax-free cash because it is money which you already 'possess'! You keep the right to remain in your home for the rest of your life, although the debt and any accrued interest will reduce the value of the estate you leave when you die

Do you qualify?

The main criterion is your age. The minimum age is 55 – in joint cases both must be aged 55 or over. Your home is the security for the loan so the lender concentrates its qualification on that. Lenders prefer conventional construction, in a good state of repair and worth at least £70,000. The tenure can be freehold or leasehold.

Your income, savings and investments are irrelevant. You could be a millionaire or a pauper, it makes no difference. Your health is not a consideration either, except in a potentially positive way - if you suffer from a serious illness or condition which could shorten your life expectancy you may be able to release more equity than if you were healthier.

Is it safe?

The sale of equity release plans is fully regulated by the Financial Conduct Authority (FCA). Financial advisers and brokers must be formally qualified, and must follow strict rules to ensure that any particular plan is suitable for you, the potential purchaser.

If you have a dispute with your adviser you have the added protection of the Financial Services Compensation Scheme which can offer financial redress should you suffer financial loss as a result of the advice given. In addition, the Equity Release Council monitors lenders and brokers and insists the lender's mortgage offer includes:

- A no negative equity guarantee – the loan can never be larger than the value of your home
- Right to reside – you can remain in your home for life
- You can move to another property, perhaps to downsize or be closer to your family (subject to the new property being acceptable to your lender)
- Your contract with the lender will not be invoked until you receive independent advice from a solicitor of your choice, ensuring that the plan offered fulfils your requirements

What can I use the money for?

No-one can tell you how to spend the money you release from your home. Currently the most popular uses are:

- Repayment of an existing mortgage
- Home Improvements (perhaps a new kitchen or conservatory)
- Repayment of Debts such as credit card loans
- A gift to a child or grandchild (e.g. to help them onto the housing ladder or help pay their university fees)
- To give your offspring a 'living inheritance' which you yourself can watch, enjoy and see the results of
- To finance the purchase of a new car
- To pay for that "dream holiday" which was never possible before
- To enhance your pension and enjoy a better standard of living

Types of Equity release schemes

There are two main types of scheme – Lifetime Mortgages and Home Reversion. Each has advantages and disadvantages.

Lifetime Mortgages

These are similar to conventional Interest Only mortgages, except that there are no monthly repayments to make. Instead, interest due is added to the balance of the loan, which therefore gets bigger over time. Hence these mortgages are sometimes referred to as Roll-Up mortgages.

Typically you would be able to borrow between 17% and 56% of the value of your home, depending on your and your partner's ages - possibly enhanced if you suffer from an illness or have a condition, which limits your life expectancy.

Do I have to take all the cash immediately?

No. You can agree a loan amount with a lender, but take a smaller initial lump sum. Should you require further money in the future, because a larger loan was agreed at the outset, you just need to ask for more when you want it. This is referred to as Drawdown or Cash Reserve. The advantage of this is that you only incur interest on the cash you have actually borrowed, the 'balance' remaining in your reserve attracts no interest at all unless and until you draw down a further amount.

For example, suppose a couple qualify for a lifetime mortgage of £100,000. They decide that they do not need the whole amount now as it exceeds the cost of their home improvement project, so they 'withdraw' £30,000 as an initial advance. Interest will accrue on the £30,000 but the balance of £70,000 is retained indefinitely in a reserve.

If you utilise a Drawdown facility, but never take any further money beyond your initial withdrawal there are no costs or penalties. You are not obliged to borrow if you do not want to. The peace of mind of just having the facility available is enough for many borrowers.

Is the Interest Rate fixed?

Yes. The interest rate can be fixed for life giving you the certainty that whatever happens in the future, the agreed rate will not change.

If you decide to take a further advance under the Drawdown facility, then that too can be on a fixed interest rate, although it may not be at the original rate. Rather, it will be the rate prevailing at the time the drawdown is taken, which may be higher or lower than the original rate.

Flexible Options

These mortgages allow the borrower to make interest payments and/or capital repayments, during the term of the mortgage. The advantage, clearly, is that you can avoid or mitigate the build-up of compound interest. For example, if you pay interest for the term of the mortgage, the loan will not get any bigger than the original amount borrowed, and any eventual inheritance is safeguarded.

But you do not have to commit to making these payments forever. Should circumstances change, or you decide you no longer wish to continue making payments, you can just stop making them. There is no adverse effect, other than that the interest which accrues from then on will be added to the loan.

Now that the concept of Lifetime mortgages has become very popular there are a myriad of options available in the marketplace. Equity Release with Buy-to-Let property, and the option of Inheritance Protection of part of the property are just two of the latest variants to appear.

With new products coming to the market, with more features and options, there is a huge choice enabling solutions tailor-made to individual needs. To explore these and find the one that best suit your needs and circumstances you need to engage a professional adviser who will provide you with a personal illustration.

Home Reversion Plans

This method of releasing equity does not involve any type of mortgage or other borrowing. Instead, with a reversion plan you sell all or part of your home, for a tax-free lump sum, to an investment company. In addition, the purchasing company will give you a legal guarantee that you can continue to live in the property as a tenant (rent free or for a nominal rent) for the rest of your life, or until you go into full-time residential care.

Because you are guaranteed occupancy for an indefinite period you will not receive the full market value for the property (or part thereof) but a percentage of it according to your age and gender. When the property is sold on your death or you move into full-time residential care, the investment company receives a share of the proceeds, corresponding to the percentage share they originally purchased. The balance will go to your estate. If, for example, you sold half of your house to the investment company on its eventual sale your estate will receive 50% of the sum obtained.

An advantage of home reversion is that you know exactly what proportion of the property is yours, but you do not own it 100%. If the house increases in value, you will only receive part of that, according to the percentage that you own.

Lifetime Mortgages, as described above, far exceed reversion plans in their popularity as you always maintain 100% ownership and it is relatively easy if you want to downsize at a later date. This can be problematic with home reversion as you will need to sell part of the house, making it very difficult to find a buyer. Also, with a reversion plan, there is no Drawdown option available.

Are there any tax implications?

There are no negative tax implications – all monies released from the equity in your home are totally free from any tax. However, be aware that taking equity release may affect any Pension Credit or Council Tax Relief you receive.

Happily, there may be a positive tax implication if your estate will be subject to Inheritance Tax (IHT). Currently (2019) IHT is payable if your estate exceeds £325,000, or £650,000 if you outlive your spouse or civil partner (plus any Residence Nil Band Rate which may apply – see page 29 for details). If your estate exceeds the relevant figure then the excess will be subject to IHT at the rate of 40%, but if you have taken equity release, the gross repayment due on your death (comprising the initial sum or sums released, plus accrued interest) will be deductible from the gross value of the estate, for IHT purposes. Therefore, for every £1000 deductible the tax saving will be £400.

N.B. See also Inheritance Tax and Estate Planning in Section 1 above, in this chapter.

Other Options

By far the easiest, and often cheapest, way to release equity is to sell your home and buy a cheaper one. This can often be achieved practically as you may not need a large house (or garden) in your later years and can downsize while retaining the standard of accommodation you are used to.

However, this option is not without cost – estate agents' fees, legal fees, removal costs and, of course Stamp Duty on your purchase can, all together, add up to a substantial sum.

Other options might include renting out part of the house, although the consequent lack of privacy would be a disadvantage.

Finally, if your children (as the eventual beneficiaries of your estate) are in a position to do so they might step in and help you out financially, thus protecting their inheritance and enabling you to remain in your home.

Further Information

Equity release requires a good deal of thought and consideration. The notes above are intended only as a short introductory guide to the subject. Every Equity Release is a bespoke solution for that individual or couple and advice should be sought from a specialist equity release broker.

As AgeUK advocates "Before you take out any (equity release) scheme, it is vital that you seek independent financial and legal advice".

3. Long-Term Residential Care

The possibility of moving into a long-term residential care home is one which potentially faces us all.

Local Authority or NHS Funding?

When you go into a care home for 'social' rather than 'health' reasons it is the local authority, not the NHS, which is the 'controlling' authority and it is they who will determine whether you will be asked to contribute towards the costs, and if so, by how much.

Please note that this publication deals only with local authority funding.

Residential care (for social reasons) is not provided free of charge in the UK unless you have a relatively low amount of savings and low income. This section briefly outlines the extent to which you may have to contribute to your care, and the implications of this.

Whether or not you pay, and how much, is determined by your income and savings. There is a fixed 'Upper Limit' to the amount of savings you can have and still receive local authority funding towards the cost. This limit is adjustable upwards in any year, but it has not been altered since 2010. A number of changes have been mooted since that time but volatile and extraordinary economic and political events in the interim (principally the financial crash and Brexit) have prevented enactment of such changes.

The Upper limit is different in each of the four home countries. Currently (year 2019/20) the Upper Limit is £23,250 in England and Northern Ireland, £28,000 in Scotland and £50,000 in Wales. If you have savings in excess of the relevant amount you will have to pay the full cost of your care until such time as your savings fall to the Limit, when the local authority will start to contribute.

If you own your own home its value will be counted as 'capital' and considered part of your savings. This usually means that you will be expected to sell it to pay the fees. However, your home will not be counted as capital, and therefore not have to be sold, if your spouse (or civil partner) lives in the house, or a close relative under the age of 16 or over the age of 60 (or a relative of any age who is incapacitated) needs to go on living there.

Sometimes the local authority may also ignore the value of the property if it is the permanent home of someone like a carer. This is at the discretion of the local authority.

In all other circumstances you will have to sell your home to realise its value to pay for the care fees. The only exception to this is that, if you do not wish to sell your house, the authority may allow you to defer payment of your contribution, to be paid in full when the house is eventually sold (in effect granting you an interest-free loan).

Calculating your Contribution

If your savings (including the value of your home) amount to more than the Upper Limit you will be liable to pay all the care fees, regardless of your income.

If and when your savings fall below (or equal) this Upper Limit the local authority will step in and make a contribution to the fees. Both your savings and your income will be taken into account when calculating the contribution (see illustrated example below).

So far as your savings are concerned there is also a Lower Limit which, like the Upper Limit, is adjustable upward each year, but which has not changed since 2010. Currently the Lower Limit is £14,250 in England and Northern Ireland, and £17,500 in Scotland. In Wales there is no Lower Limit.

If savings are below the Lower Limit they are ignored for calculation purposes. However, for any savings you have which are between the Lower and Upper Limits will form part of the calculation of your contribution to fees. For each £250 (or part thereof) of savings you have above the lower but below the upper limit you will be deemed to receive an income of £1 per week.

So, for example, if you live in England and have savings totaling £14,750 (£500 above the lower limit) your notional income will be £2 per week.

To this notional income is added all your other income from pensions (state, occupational or personal) and any income from benefits, to arrive at a figure for your total weekly income.

When deciding on the level of contribution you must make towards your care fees the local authority must always leave you with some spending money. This is called a Personal Expenses Allowance (or PEA). Again the PEA differs across the four countries – in England and Northern Ireland it is set at £24.90 per week, in Scotland it is £27.75 and in Wales £29.50.

Subtracting the Personal Expenses Allowance from total weekly income gives the level of contribution the local authority will require from you to cover your care costs, up to the full amount of the fees.

Illustrative Example (financial year 2019/20)

Suppose a person in residential care in England has savings of £15,600, state pension of £145 per week, and a small private pension of £25 per week. What contribution to their care home fees will they have to make?

Their notional income from savings will be calculated as follows:

£15,600 less the lower limit of £14250 = £1350. 1350 divided by 250 = 5.4. Therefore the notional income from savings is £6 per week (the figure is always rounded up).

The required contribution calculation;

	£
Notional Savings	6.00
plus State Pension	145.00
Private Pension	25.00
Total weekly income	176.00
Less Personal Allowance	24.90
Required Weekly Contribution	151.10 per week

Any shortfall between the contribution and the actual care home fees is paid by the local authority.

In Wales (unlike in England, Scotland or Northern Ireland) there is no Lower Limit and therefore no calculation of notional income to be included when assessing the level of income. Apart from that (and the different Upper Limit) there is no difference in the system of assessment in Wales.

Giving away property and savings

Note that it is illegal to give property or savings to another person in order to qualify for financial help from your local authority. Such actions are referred to as Deprivation of Assets and if the local authority suspects that this has occurred they may try to reclaim the fees

If you give away your home you may lose control over what happens to it. Even though you may feel protected if you give it to your children or other family members you may have no legal rights if things change.

N.B. The above is a brief and simplified explanation of the means of calculating an individual's contribution to the costs of residential care, when needed for social reasons, in the four home countries. The figures stated are subject to change from year to year.

It is generally accepted that the current means of providing and funding residential care is inappropriate and not fit for purpose in the UK in the 21st century. There have been attempts in the last several years to introduce reforms but these have not succeeded due to political and economic reasons. Nevertheless, though there is a growing consensus that reform is overdue it is impossible to forecast when that might happen.

4. Funding a Funeral

The cost of funerals has risen inexorably over the past several years and the trend shows no sign of abating.

According to the government-funded Money Advice Service the average cost of a funeral in 2019 was £3757, representing an increase of some 37% over the last ten years (in 2004 the average cost was less than £2000). These figures exclude 'extras' such as flowers, catering, headstone, death notices, venue hire, etc.

There are wide regional variations within the above quoted average figure. Generally, burials are more expensive than cremations, sometimes markedly so in areas where land is in short supply. For example, a standard cremation in Wales in 2019 cost around £3163, compared with an average cost of £6479 for a burial in London in the same year.

Generally, the costs of the funeral will be charged against, and ultimately paid by, your estate. If you have the available funds you may want to consider purchasing a Funeral Bond (also known as a Funeral Plan).

Funeral Bonds

It is possible to pay for one's funeral in advance by purchasing a Funeral Bond. This has the advantage of letting you purchase at today's prices so that you beat any future inflationary rise.

A further advantage is that the existence of a pre-paid bond will help reduce the stress and grief your family will be suffering on your death, by removing the question of funeral arrangements and payment from the immediate equation.

Your pre-payment is guaranteed and ring-fenced in a trust fund. Bonds are offered by most of the large funeral directors in the UK but you should shop around and check which aspects are guaranteed not to incur additional charges, as there is some variation. Usually prices are only guaranteed for cremations, due to the continuing shortage (and hence increasing costs) of burial grounds.

Most bonds offer a choice of funeral type, from simple through to elaborate. It is also possible to plan a bespoke funeral (i.e. draw up an advance funeral directive) and fund it with a bond. There is no limit on age. Anyone over 18 can purchase a bond on their own or on another's behalf. The age of the nominated person is not limited in any way and no medical examination is required, or indeed any information other than the name and gender of the nominee.

With some providers of bonds it is also possible to pay by instalments. If death occurs before the final instalment has been paid the funeral will be carried out as specified, and the balance due paid out of the proceeds of the estate.

Alternative Funding – An Over 50's Assurance policy

If you are concerned that your estate may not have sufficient funds to cover your funeral expenses, you may want to consider taking out a whole of life or fixed-term assurance policy which will pay out a guaranteed lump sum on your death. Such policies are often marketed as "Over 50's plans".

Setting up such an assurance policy to fund the funeral will enable undertakers to be paid promptly (as their terms of business often require) and thereby avoid the potential problem which you family may otherwise face, that of waiting for probate to be granted to pay the cost out of the estate.

These policies are available from leading UK insurance companies and are specifically aimed at those in the age range 50 – 80. Typically no medical examinations or declarations are required and acceptance into the plan is guaranteed.

If you take out such a policy the ultimate usage of the eventual payout is up to you – it does not have to be used to pay funeral expenses and can be used for any purpose.

N.B. It is recommended that independent financial advice be sought, as in other financial matters, to ensure that such a policy is best suited to your needs and circumstances.

Part D - Checklist

Your Will

- Have you drawn up a Will?
- Have you made a directory of your digital assets and do your family know where it is located?

  When did you last update the directory?

Reviewing your Will

- When did you draw up your Will?
- When did you last review it?
- Have there been legislative or tax changes in the interim?
- Has your family/circle of friends changed since you wrote your Will?
- Have you changed your mind about your chosen beneficiaries?
- Do you need to review your Will with your solicitor?

Registering your Will

- Have you registered your Will to ensure it will be found after you die?

Organ/Body Donation

- If you would like others to live after your death, have you taken steps to let it be known you would like to donate your organs?
- Do you want to leave your body for research or training purposes? If so, have you made the necessary arrangements?

Lasting Power of Attorney (Personal Welfare)

- Do you want to nominate someone to act on your behalf in terns of your medical treatment and personal welfare should you become mentally or physically incapacitated in the future?

Lasting Power of Attorney (Property & Affairs)

- Do you want to nominate someone to act on your behalf in financial matters if you should become incapable of doing so yourself?

Advance Decision (Living Will)

- Have you made an Advance Decision which specifies the medical treatment you would wish to receive should you become incapacitated and unable to communicate your wishes to your medical team and your family?

Advance Funeral Directive

- Have you decided whether you want to be buried or cremated, what type of funeral you want, what music should be played or poems read, etc.?
- Are your family or next of kin aware of where your Advance Directive is located?

Funding the Funeral

- Have you purchased a bond so the funeral is paid for in advance?
- Have you put aside (or insured for) a sum to pay for your funeral?

Part E - A Final Thought

This book has been written for a simple purpose – to encourage you, the reader, to think about your later years and to contemplate and prepare for the period leading up to the end of your life, and death itself.

The prospect, for most of us, is not a pleasant one. As human beings we have a tendency to push the thought of death aside. We know it will eventually happen, but we prefer to put it to the backs of our minds and not think about it.

However, the consequences of not devoting thought and not taking action will almost certainly be negative, both for ourselves and for our families.

When loved ones die, those who grieve want, indeed deserve, to know how to mark their passing and how to administer and share in any assets left behind. Not to leave clear instructions in these matters can only cause them more grief and worry at best, and perhaps bitter family strife and division at worst.

We live in a time when, compared to previous generations, most of us can look forward to long lives in retirement. For example, life expectancy at age 65 in 2015 was 79.2 years for men and 82.9 years for women (source: Office for National Statistics).

This is good news of course, but with it comes the potential price of failing health and capacity – about 1 in 5 men can anticipate spending the last period of their lives in some form of residential care, and 1 in 3 women. A significant and growing number of elderly people will suffer some form of mental and/or physical incapacity during their final years.

For our own sakes, if not for others, it is surely prudent to make practical arrangements for such potential occurrences whilst we can, utilising some of the means outlined in this book. By so doing we may improve the quality of the last period of our lives, and at the same time, mitigate the pain and worry, and eventual grief suffered by our family when we pass away.

Part F -
Further Information

Listed here are the names, addresses and contact details of organisations which may offer useful additional information on various aspects of the topics included in this book.

Will Registration

Certainty National Will Register
The Chapel, Chapel Lane, Lapworth, Warwicks, B94 6EU
Tel: 0330 100 3660
www.nationalwillregister.co.uk

Certainty offers anyone the opportunity to register their Will, for a modest one-off fee, so that its location can be determined after death.

Equity Release

Equity Release Council
The Old Rectory, Church Lane, Thornby, NN6 8SN
Tel: 0300 012 0239
www.equityreleasecouncil.com

The ERC is a trade organisation representing the equity release industry. Its members include lenders, financial advisers, solicitors, surveyors and other professionals. The ERC code of practice includes a "no negative equity guarantee" which ensures that money borrowed by the home-owner, plus interest accrued, will never exceed the value of the home.

Long-Term Residential Care

Directgov
Web: http://www.direct.gov.uk/en/CaringForSomeone

Directgov is the Government's online information service which can be accessed via the internet, telephone or your television screen. It carries advice and information on many issues including the question of funding long-term residential care.

AgeUK
Tavis House, 1-6 Tavistock Square, London, WC1H 9NA
Tel: 0800 678 1602
www.ageuk.org.uk

The organisation provides help and advice through its website, its advisers and through publications, including advice on residential care.

Elderly Accommodation Counsel (EAC)
Suite A, 202 Lambeth Road, London SE1 7JW
Tel: 020 7820 1682
www.housingcare.org

Elderly Accommodation Counsel (EAC) is a national charity that aims to help older people make informed choices about meeting their housing and care needs. The website contains a wealth of information on the whole topic of residential care and also has a national database of homes.

Funeral Planning

National Association of Funeral Directors
618 Warwick Road, Solihull, B91 1AA
Tel: 0121 711 1343
www.nafd.org.uk

A national association of funeral directors who all adhere to a strict code of practice in respect of standards of service, marketing and advertising, price information and estimates. The association offers a pre-paid funeral plan.

National Society of Allied and Independent Funeral Directors (SAIF)
SAIF Business Centre, 3 Bullfields, Sawbridgeworth, CM21 9DB
Tel: 0345 230 6777 / 01279 726 777
www.saif.org.uk

Members operate within a strict code of practice in respect of standards of service - has about 700 members nationwide, mostly small and family firms.

Compassion in Dying
181 Oxford Street
London W1D 2JT
Tel: 0800 999 2434
Web: www.compassionindying.org.uk

This charity, a sister organisation to Dignity in Dying, contains helpful information on how to prepare for the process of dying, including a format for an Advance Decision which is downloadable free of charge.

The Natural Death Centre
In the Hill House, Watley Lane, Twyford, Winchester, SO21 1QX
Tel: 01962 712 690
www.naturaldeath.org.uk

This is a charitable project which aims to support those dying at home, and their carers, and to help people arrange inexpensive, family-organised and environmentally-friendly funerals. It maintains a list of natural burial grounds and also offers free information and a number of useful publications.

Humanists UK
39 Moreland Street, London, EC1V 8BB
Tel: 020 7324 3060
www.humanism.org.uk

Humanists UK (formerly known as the British Humanists Association) is a charitable organisation which promotes humanism and aims to represent people who seek to live good lives without religious or superstitious beliefs. It maintains a register of officiants who are qualified to perform non-religious funerals. The website contains a search facility to find an officiant in your area.

Marine Management Organisation (for Burials at Sea)
Marine Management Organisation, Hampshire Court,
Newcastle-upon-Tyne, NE4 7YH
Tel: 0300 123 1032
www.gov.uk/government/organisations/marine-management-organisation

If you wish to be buried at sea this is the body to whom application has to be made.

Bereavement Advice Centre
Heron House, Timothy's Bridge Road, Stratford-Upon-Avon, CV37 9BX
Tel: 0800 634 9494
www.bereavementadvice.org

The BAC is a free web-based information service provided by Co-op Legal Services. It carries comprehensive information and advice on the many issues which affect the recently bereaved.

Organ/Body Donation

NHS Organ Donor Register
Fox Den Road, Stoke Gifford, Bristol, BS34 8RR
Tel: 0117 975 7575 / 0300 123 23 23
www.organdonation.nhs.uk

NHS Blood and Transplant (NHSBT) operates the UK Organ Donor Register. The website contains lots of useful and interesting information and offers the facility to "sign up" online.

The Human Tissue Authority
151 Buckingham Palace Road, London SW1W 9SZ
Tel: 020 7269 1900
www.hta.gov.uk

The HTA is the organisation through whom application must be made for donation of one's body for medical research or training. It does not collect or receive bodies or other human materials, but licenses and inspects the organisations that do. Details of your local medical school are available on the website or by calling the above number.

Lasting Power of Attorney

Office of the Public Guardian
PO Box 16185, Birmingham, B2 2WH
Tel: 300 456 0300
Web: www.gov.uk/government/organisations/office-of-the-public-guardian

The OPG is part of the Department for Constitutional Affairs and acts as the administrative arm of the Court of Protection. The site has a number of downloadable guides and other useful information.

The OPG is the body which is responsible for registering Lasting Powers of Attorney, and it also deals with applications for the appointment of Deputies to administer the affairs of persons who are incapacitated and have not appointed an attorney.

General Information

Money Advice Service
Holborn Centre, 120 Holborn, London EC1N 2TD
Tel: 0800 138 7777
www.moneyadviceservice.co.uk

An independent organisation established by Parliament, the Money Advice Service offers free and impartial advice online and by phone on money matters generally, including retirement planning, equity release and residential care.

HM Revenue & Customs - Inheritance Tax (IHT) information & advice
Helpline: 0300 200 3300
Web: www.gov.uk/inheritance-tax

Financial Ombudsman Service
Exchange Tower, Harbour Exchange, London E14 9SR
Tel: 0800 023 4567
www.financial-ombudsman.org.uk

Set up by Parliament the Financial Ombudsman Service is the UK's official expert in sorting out problems with financial services. It is available to consumers generally and can offer general advice. It also has extensive powers to police the manner and methods by which services are offered and administered by financial institutions.

Appendices

In this section of **Life**Holder we include further information and guidance on the topics covered in the previous two sections:

Guide for Executors is written for lay individuals who have agreed to be nominated as an executor to a Will and is a brief summary of the duties required and responsibilities involved. It describes all the steps and actions required, from registering the death up to the drawing-up of a final account of the estate.

Guide for Donors is written for those who are considering setting up a Lasting Power of Attorney and explains how a Power can be set up, giving one or more attorneys powers to handle their (the donor's) affairs.

Guide for Attorneys is written for lay individuals who may be asked, by a relative or friend, to become their attorney, under a Lasting Power of Attorney, and contains a brief summary of the duties and responsibilities of an attorney so appointed.

Living Will (Advance Decision) - a short format simple example of a Living Will is shown here.

Appendix 1 - Guide for Executors

An Executor is responsible for putting into effect the terms and wishes laid out in someone's Will, and winding up their affairs. In brief, an executor is required to:

Register the death, **Arrange** the funeral, **Secure** the home and property of the deceased, **Obtain** a grant of Probate, **Gather** details of all the assets and liabilities of the deceased, **Collect** in, or realise, all the assets of the deceased, **Pay** all debts and expenses attributable to the deceased, **Distribute** the cash and assets from the estate according to the Will, **Transfer** funds remaining which are to be held for children in a Trust to the named trustees and, finally, **Draw** up an account to show how all the financial aspects of the estate have been dealt with

Registering a Death

When someone dies, the death needs to be registered within 5 days at the register office in the district where the death has occurred. All large towns have a registry office and some are to be found in smaller conurbations.

Most deaths are registered by a relative of the deceased. The registrar will normally only allow others to register the death (such as someone present at the death, or the person who found the body if death did not occur in hospital) if there are no relatives available to do it

When registering you will be asked for the following details:

- date and place of death
- name and surname of the deceased, and maiden name if applicable
- date and place of birth
- occupation

- name and occupation of spouse or civil partner, as appropriate
- usual address
- details of any pension or benefits the deceased received from public funds
- date of birth of any surviving spouse or civil partner

The only document you need is the medical certificate of cause of death, issued by the doctor who pronounced the death. If possible you should also take the deceased's NHS medical card.

If the death has been reported to the coroner, the registrar will need additional documentation from them before the death can be registered.

After completing the formalities you will have the opportunity of buying one or more **death certificates**. Almost certainly you will need more than one as each organisation you need to inform of the death (such as the deceased's bank, building society) will require to see a copy.

The registrar will also issue a **certificate for the burial or cremation** of the body. This should be passed to the funeral director since the funeral cannot proceed without it. In cases where a death has been reported to the coroner he or she will normally issue the certificate for burial or cremation. You will also need to complete a certificate for social security benefits and send this to your local Benefits office so that the Department for Work and Pensions can deal with all matters pertaining to any benefits and state pensions.

Tell Us Once service

This is offered by most local authorities on behalf of the Department for Work and Pensions. It is free to use, and can save you considerable time and effort. Basically the service allows you to inform central and local government services of the death at one time rather than having to write to or telephone the appropriate bodies, or even attend meetings.

The service, in most cases, will be offered to you by the registrar, immediately on registration of the death. He or she will check with you which government services need to be notified, and will then effect the procedure immediately.

Documents or details you will need to take to the registry include the following (as appropriate):

- NI number and date of birth of the deceased
- Their passport (or passport number) and place of birth
- Driving licence or driving licence number
- Blue Badge (if relevant)
- Details of state pension and benefits
- Death Certificate (if not completing Tell Us Once at the time of registration)

If you are the next of kin and receive state benefits, these may change so you need your own NI number available when using the service.

Arranging the Funeral

Sometimes the deceased will have expressed their wishes as to the method of disposal of the body (burial or cremation) and their preferences for the funeral service. They may have left informal instructions with a friend or relative, or made a more formal statement by making an Advance Funeral Directive.

Whatever the situation, you will need to consult with family members, particularly any surviving spouse or civil partner, so you are sure that you are acceding to the wishes of the deceased and those of the family.

Securing the Home and Property of the Deceased

If the deceased leaves a surviving spouse, civil partner or other family member living in their home you will not be required to secure it! However, if they lived alone it will be necessary to do so. Until the home is sold, or the lease formally given up, it will be your responsibility to keep it secure.

You will, however, in all cases need to locate and take possession of all relevant documents including bank statements, share certificates, savings account books, cheque books, credit and debit cards, tax records and indeed everything relating to the financial aspects of the recent life of the deceased.

Obtaining Probate

In order to get authority to deal with the deceased's estate the executor has to obtain a legal document (called a Grant of Representation or Probate) from the Probate Registry, which is part of HM Courts Service. [If no executors are named in the Will, or the person has died intestate, the Grant of Representation is called Letters of Administration.] Without a grant those organisations holding money in the deceased's name (such as banks, building societies, insurance companies etc.) will not be inclined to release the money to you. Also you cannot sell or transfer a property held in the deceased's sole name without a grant. Having a grant is proof that you may collect the money or sell the property.

As an executor you can apply for probate yourself. The process involves obtaining and completing various forms and completing and returning them to the Probate Registry and to HM Revenue and Customs along with the original Will, an original copy of the death certificate, the necessary fees, and possibly other documents. You must then attend an interview at the Probate Registry.

Not surprisingly most people prefer to appoint a solicitor to apply for the grant on their behalf. It is much simpler and you are not required to attend a personal interview.

Note: If the estate is small* it can be distributed without a grant of probate. Banks and building societies will usually release small amounts of money on receipt of a copy of the death certificate. Also, accounts held in joint names can usually be transferred to the surviving account holder without probate.

** Legally, small is defined as less than £5000, a figure which was determined in an act of parliament in 1965. Adding inflation to that figure increases it substantially so that, in practice, banks will apply a more generous limit before insisting on probate. Lloyds Bank, for example, applies a limit of £50,000. Other banks may vary from that figure but most now ignore the legal limit of £5000*

Write to Relevant Organisations

The main task at this stage is to ascertain the value of the assets of the deceased, including obtaining valuations of any property or other non-liquid assets. The latter may, of course involve seeking the opinion of experts such as estate agents.

You will also need to ascertain the extent of any liabilities such as utility bills, mortgages or loans.

Given the ability to calculate the net assets you will now be in a position to assess whether any inheritance tax may be due and the likely amounts that beneficiaries will be entitled to receive.

Note that if you use the Tell Us Once service (see above under Registering a Death) you will not need to write to any national or local government department or agency. They will contact you if required.

Realise and Collect the Assets and Pay Liabilities and Expenses

Most of the organisations holding money on behalf of the deceased will require to see a copy of the grant of probate and some may also want to see the death certificate.

You will need to set up a separate bank account to receive monies due and to pay liabilities and any expenses such as funeral costs. Specifically, you will need to establish the tax position with HM Revenue and Customs. A payment may be due, or a refund. If the estate was large enough inheritance tax will also be payable.

Distribute Cash and Assets to Beneficiaries

When the final net value after tax has been determined, the money and other assets should be distributed according to the wishes of the deceased as expressed in the Will.

Any legacies should also be paid and any physical assets stipulated in the Will handed over.

Transfer Funds in Respect of any Trusts

If the Will directed that any trusts be set up, for example for the benefit of any children, the monies should be handed over to the named trustees.

Accounting Record

An account of how the financial aspects of the estate have been dealt with should now be drawn up so that any interested parties may see for themselves how the estate has been distributed.

You may wish, in particular, to send a copy of the account to the major beneficiaries. Note too that HM Revenue and Customs may wish to see a copy.

Help and Assistance

Winding up an estate can be a protracted and time consuming process. For this reason most people choose to arrange for professional help and advice.

Appendix 2 - Guide for Donors

What is A Lasting Power of Attorney?

An LPA is a legal document which enables you (the donor) to nominate another person (an attorney) to deal with your affairs in the event of you becoming incapacitated. The attorney should be someone you can trust implicitly. Very often a close relative is chosen, but an attorney can be almost anyone provided they are over the age of 18 and not bankrupt.

Types of LPA

There are two types of LPA. One deals with Property & Affairs (financial matters) and the other deals with Personal Welfare (health and social issues). It is a matter of personal choice whether to draw up a Power of each type, or just one, or neither.

Both are regulated by the Office of the Public Guardian (OPG) a government controlled body and the procedures for establishing them are broadly similar. Each must be made on a statutory form, available from solicitors and legal stationers or online. Each must be registered by the OPG before the provisions can take effect.

The following paragraphs refer to the Property & Affairs LPA. However, all procedures and descriptions also apply to a Personal Welfare LPA. The one significant difference on the statutory forms is that on the Personal Welfare version you, the donor, are required to state and confirm whether or not you wish to give your attorney(s) the authority to give or refuse consent to life-sustaining treatment on your behalf.

What is the Purpose of an LPA?

An LPA is a precautionary step taken by the donor in case he or she considers they may become incapacitated, or otherwise prevented from handling their own affairs, in the future. It literally donates the power to act on your behalf, to the attorney.

An LPA is therefore a very powerful document. As the donor you can donate general powers, giving control over your financial affairs and empowering the attorney to act generally on your behalf and in your interests. Or you may choose to donate a specific power or powers, for example, to pay your bills but not to sell your assets.

Often a general power may be given with restrictions – for example, power to deal with all your property and affairs but not allowing the sale of real estate or other specific assets.

As donor it is for you to decide, perhaps with the benefit of advice from family and professional advisers, what powers you wish to donate, and in what circumstances.

Is it Safe to Make an LPA?

As stated above LPAs are very powerful instruments. Remember that the person you appoint as your attorney may have complete power over your money, savings, investments and property. If you become mentally incapable, you will be unable to check what they are doing.

When choosing your attorney, consider how well they handle their own financial affairs - Do you trust them to act in your best interests? Will they use your money solely to provide for your needs?

Safeguards

As a safeguard you can appoint more than one attorney (see below). You can also add conditions to the LPA when you make it, for example, requiring the attorney to make regular reports to your solicitor or your accountant.

There are also safeguards included in the procedures for establishing an LPA. A pre-condition is that you must discuss your intent to set up a Power with someone you know (but excluding your spouse, any relatives or carers, or your chosen attorney – in short, anyone who could potentially benefit from a situation where you give a power of attorney).

If you do not know any suitable individual personally you may choose a solicitor, or other professional person. The person you choose to discuss the matter with has then to sign a document called 'Statement of certificate provider' confirming that, in their opinion, you are aware of the purpose of the LPA and that no undue pressure is being put on you to create the Power.

You can also nominate, on the statutory form, up to five people to be notified when an application is made to register the Power with the Public Guardian. This is a safeguard since any of these people named will have an opportunity to object to the registration of the LPA.

Joint Attorneys

It is possible to appoint more than one attorney. This can be as a safeguard but sometimes joint attorneys are appointed because the donor wants, as well as a close relative or friend, a professional person such as an accountant or a solicitor, to ensure the duties are carried out correctly and efficiently.

Attorneys may be joint, or joint and several. Appointing joint attorneys means that all decisions and actions taken have to be taken jointly (for example, all their signatures will be required on cheques). This can be inconvenient and, if one attorney cannot act for some reason, or dies, the power will fail.

Appointing attorneys jointly and severally means they can act separately or together. This is clearly more flexible. If the donor wishes, restrictions can be imposed (for example, by requiring that all attorneys have to sign for transactions worth over £1000).

Can Attorneys Charge for Their Services?

Non-professional attorneys are not expected to charge for their services, although they may be reimbursed (at your option) for reasonable expenses.

Professional attorneys such as solicitors, accountants or banks are entitled to charge.

Registering the LPA

By law your LPA must be registered with the Public Guardian before you lose the mental capacity to make decisions for yourself. Until it is registered the Power cannot be used. Your nominees (noted on the statutory form) will be contacted by the Guardian when registration is requested. If any object to the registration the Guardian will investigate the circumstances and then make a ruling.

It takes at least 35 days from the date of application before the LPA is registered, to allow time for any objections.

Once registration is approved, the LPA will be sealed on every page by the Public Guardian and returned to the attorney. From then on the attorney must answer to the Court of Protection if anyone questions their actions and the LPA cannot be ended without the agreement of the Court or the OPG.

The institutions with whom the attorney will have to deal (such as bank, building society, nursing home, Benefits Agency, HM Revenue & Customs etc.) will require sight of the registered document before they will act on the attorney's instructions.

Duties & Responsibilities of an Attorney

The appointed attorney is bound to act in the best interests of the donor and consider their needs and wishes. He/she must not take advantage of the donor's situation to gain any benefit for themselves and they must keep your money and property separate from their own.

Can they make gifts?

An attorney has limited power to make gifts. For example, they can make seasonal gifts (e.g. at Christmas) to people to whom you might normally have made gifts. They can also make gifts, to appropriate recipients, on anniversaries such as birthdays. Or, they could make donations to any charity you might have been expected to support.

If they want to make larger gifts of money or property they must apply to the Court for permission.

Must they keep accounts?

Yes, they have a duty to keep accounts of all their dealings for the donor. They should keep a full record of all the donor's income and expenditure, together with receipts, invoices and bank statements. The Court of Protection can ask that they produce accounts at any time.

Can they sell the donor's house?

Yes, if they feel this is in the donor's best interests and provided there are no restrictions in the LPA which prevent this. They must be confident there is no reasonable chance the donor will be able to return to live at home.

The approval of the OPG or the Court is not required unless the attorney wants to buy the property themselves, or if they want to give it to someone else, or if the sale is below market value.

Can they stop acting as attorney?

Yes. Stopping to act as an attorney is known as 'disclaiming the power'. They should ask solicitors to prepare a Deed of Disclaimer.

If they are the sole attorney the usual step is for someone to apply to the Court to appoint a deputy. If there are joint attorneys and one wants to give up, the LPA can no longer be used and the donor's affairs will have to be managed in another way. If there are joint and several attorneys the remaining attorney can continue to act under the LPA but the PGO should be informed about the change.

What are the Powers of the Court of Protection?

The Court has powers to intervene in running a registered LPA if anyone suspects the attorney is not acting in the donor's best interests. It may also ask them to produce accounts, answer for any dealings, provide documents or information, or explain why they took certain actions. Ultimately the Court has power to suspend or end their duties.

Appendix 3 - Guide for Attorneys

What is a Lasting Power of Attorney?

An LPA is a legal document nominating one or more attorneys to deal with the affairs of another person (known as a donor). The attorney is chosen by the donor as someone they can trust implicitly and very often it is a close relative. They can, however, be almost anyone provided they are over the age of 18 and not bankrupt at the time they sign

What is the Purpose of an LPA?

An LPA is a precautionary step taken by the donor in case he or she considers they may be mentally incapacitated in the future, or otherwise prevented from handling their own affairs. It literally donates their power to act on their own behalf, to you as an attorney.

An LPA can therefore be a very powerful document. The donor will decide, perhaps with the benefit of advice from family and professional advisers, what powers they wish to donate, and in what circumstances. You need to decide whether you wish to accept the responsibility of becoming an attorney.

Types of LPA

There are two types of LPA. One deals with Property and Affairs (general financial issues) and the other deals with Personal Welfare (health and social issues).

If you are appointed an attorney under an LPA which deals with the donor's Property and Affairs you may be called on to act for them and on their behalf to organise their finances, pay their bills, even perhaps to sell their property.

Sometimes the donor will donate general powers, giving you control over their financial affairs and empowering you to act generally on their behalf and in their interests. In other circumstances the donor may donate a specific power or powers, for example, to pay their bills but not to sell their assets.

If you are appointed an attorney under an LPA which deals with the donor's Personal Welfare you may be required to take decisions about their future healthcare, living arrangements, even to decide on whether or not to give or refuse consent to life-sustaining treatment on their behalf.

The donor may choose to give you general powers or they may elect to impose restrictions or conditions.

Joint Attorneys

Sometimes the donor will appoint more than one attorney. This can be as a safeguard, because an LPA can be a very powerful tool as has been noted. Sometimes it is because the donor wants, as well as a close relative or friend, a professional person such as an accountant or a solicitor, to ensure the duties can be carried out correctly and efficiently.

Attorneys may be joint, or joint and several. If you are appointed jointly with one or more others all decisions will have to be taken jointly (for example, all your signatures will be required on cheques). This can become inconvenient and, if one attorney cannot act for some reason, or dies, the power will fail. If you are appointed jointly and severally you can act separately or together with your fellow attorney(s). This is more flexible.

Registering the LPA

An LPA (of either type) must be registered before it can take effect. Registration is completed by the Office of the Public Guardian (OPG) to whom application must be made.

In most cases the donor will have nominated other individuals (up to five) whom they wish to be advised that registration has been applied for. This is to allow any of them to object to the registration if they so wish. If any objection is made the situation will be resolved by the Court of Protection.

In the case of a Property & Affairs LPA when you make the application you will have limited powers to maintain the donor and prevent any loss to their money and property. You will have full powers (as determined by the document signed by the donor) once the LPA is registered. It will take at least 35 days from the date of application before the LPA is registered to allow time for any objections, unless the donor has not nominated anyone to be informed, in which case registration will proceed within a few days.

In the case of a Personal Welfare LPA the power cannot be used before registration and then only if the donor cannot make the required decision for themselves. The same procedure for hearing possible objections will also prevail.

Once registration is approved, the LPA will be sealed on each page with a Court of Protection stamp and returned to you. After registration you must answer to the Court of Protection if anyone questions your actions.

Many of the institutions with whom you will have to deal on the donor's behalf (such as their bank, building society, nursing homes, Benefits Agency, HM Revenue & Customs etc.) will require sight of the sealed document before they will act on your instructions.

Duties & Responsibilities of an Attorney (Property & Affairs)

As the appointed attorney you are bound to act in the best interests of the donor and consider their needs and wishes. You must not take advantage of the donor's situation to gain any benefit for yourself and you should keep the donor's money and property separate from your own. You are now managing someone else's money and have legal duties which you must respect.

Can I make gifts?
You have limited power to make gifts. For example you can make seasonal gifts (e.g. at Christmas) to people to whom the donor might normally have made gifts. You can also make gifts, to appropriate recipients, on anniversaries such as birthdays. Or, you could make donations to any charity the donor might have been expected to support.

If you want to make larger gifts of money or property, perhaps as part of Inheritance Tax Planning, you must apply to the Court for permission.

Should I keep accounts?

Yes, you have a duty to keep accounts of all your dealings for the donor, which you must be able to produce at any time. You should keep a full record of all the donor's income and expenditure, together with receipts, invoices and bank statements.

The Court of Protection can ask that you produce accounts at any time.

Can I sell the donor's house?

Yes, if you feel this is in the donor's best interests and provided there are no restrictions in the LPA which prevent this. You must be confident there is no reasonable chance the donor will be able to return to live at home.

You do not need the approval of the OPG or the Court unless you want to buy the property yourself, or you want to give it to someone else or the sale is below market value.

Duties & Responsibilities of an Attorney (Personal Welfare)

Your duties are to act on the donor's behalf in matters pertaining to their health and general well-being.

Your duties may be general and without proscribed limit in this regard, including making decisions on life-sustaining treatment, or they may be subject to restrictions or conditions, depending on what the donor has stipulated.

Can I Stop Acting as Attorney?

Yes. Stopping to act as an attorney is known as 'disclaiming the power'. If the LPA is registered you should ask a solicitor to prepare a Deed of Disclaimer. If you are the only attorney the usual step is for someone to apply to the Court to appoint a receiver.

If there are joint attorneys and one wants to give up the LPA can no longer be used and the donor's affairs will have to be managed in another way.

If there are joint and several attorneys the remaining attorney(s) can continue to act under the LPA but the OPG should be informed about the change.

It is not possible to add extra attorneys to a registered LPA.

Where Can I Get Further advice?

If you need advice on practical, financial or legal matters, you should get help from your solicitor, or other professional or financial adviser. The website of the OPG (see section F above) provides advice and information.

What are the Powers of the Court of Protection?

The Court has powers to intervene in running a registered LPA if anyone The Court has powers to intervene in running a registered LPA if anyone suspects you are not acting in the donor's best interests. It may also ask you to produce accounts, answer for your dealings, provide documents or information, or explain why you took certain actions. Ultimately the Court has power to suspend or end your duties.

What Happens When the Donor Dies?

The LPA automatically ceases on the donor's death. You should send the original LPA and the death certificate to the OPG as soon as possible. The donor's estate should now be dealt with as per the Will, or the rules of intestacy if there is no Will.

Appendix 4 - Living Will - sample format

LIVING WILL

To my doctor(s) and all those concerned with my medical well-being, this Living Will is made by me:

Name ....

of

Address ....

....

I DECLARE that if, at any time, in the future:

- I am suffering from any of the following conditions:
  - Severe immune deficiency (e.g. HIV Aids)
  - Any form of dementia
  - Severe and lasting brain damage due to injury, stroke or other cause
  - Advanced disseminated malignant disease (e.g. widespread cancer)
  - Advanced degenerative disease of the nervous system
  - Any other condition of comparable gravity; **and**
- I have become unable to participate in decisions about my health and medical care; **and**
- Two medical doctors are of the opinion that I am unlikely to recover from the condition I am suffering

THEN my wishes are:

- That I am not to be subjected to any medical treatment which is aimed at prolonging my life;
- That any distressing symptoms are to be fully controlled by appropriate analgesic or other treatment, even if such treatment may have the effect of shortening my life.

I CONSENT to anything proposed to be done in compliance with my directions as noted above and I absolve my medical and nursing attendants from any liability whatsoever arising out of such acts.

I NOMINATE
(name) ....

of

Address ....

....

....

As the person to be consulted by my medical team when, in any situation, they are uncertain as to what my intentions would be.

Signed .... Date ....

in the presence of:

WITNESSES

We testify that the maker of this Living Will signed it in our presence and confirmed that he/she understood its meaning and the possible consequences. So far as we are aware we do not stand to gain from his/her death.

Signature ....

Name ....

Address ....

....

Signature ....

Name ....

Address ....

....

Index

Notes

Notes

* 9 7 8 1 7 8 4 5 6 6 9 0 6 *

ND - #0154 - 050826 - C84 - 210/148/5 - PB - 9781784566906 - Gloss Lamination